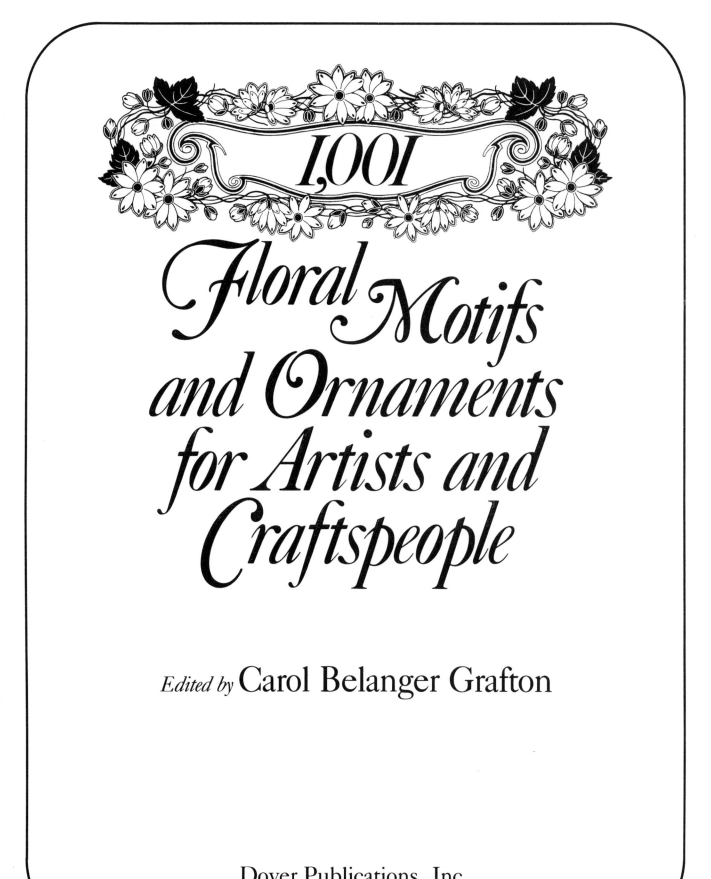

1,001

Floral Motifs and Ornaments for Artists and Craftspeople

Edited by Carol Belanger Grafton

Dover Publications, Inc.
New York

Published in Canada by General Publishing Company, Ltd.
30 Lesmill Road, Don Mills, Toronto, Ontario.
Published in the United Kingdom by Constable and Company, Ltd.

1,001 Floral Motifs and Ornaments for Artists and Craftspeople is a new work,
first published by Dover Publications, Inc., in 1987.

DOVER *Pictorial Archive* SERIES

Manufactured in the United States of America
Dover Publications, Inc.
31 East 2nd Street
Mineola, N.Y. 11501

Library of Congress Cataloging-in-Publication Data

1,001 floral motifs and ornaments for artists and craftspeople.

(Dover pictorial archive series)
1. Decoration and ornament—Plant forms. I. Grafton, Carol Belanger.
II. Title: One thousand one floral motifs and ornaments for artists and craftspeople.
III. Title: One thousand and one floral motifs and ornaments for artists
and craftspeople. IV. Series.
NK1560.A165 1987   745.4   86-24256
ISBN 0-486-25352-X

Publisher's Note

To present the designer with a resource as useful as possible, Carol Belanger Grafton has selected the designs that follow from many varied books and publications. These include: nineteenth- and early twentieth-century American, English, French, German and Spanish type catalogues (some of which reproduced earlier material); nineteenth- and twentieth-century English and American journals of the printing trade, such as *The Inland Printer*; illustrated periodicals such as *The Studio*; decorative motifs from the Middle Ages through the nineteenth century as reproduced in *L'Art pour tous* and *Formenschatz*; wood-engraved headpieces and tailpieces from nineteenth-century books; nineteenth- and twentieth-century portfolios of decorative art and floral ornament.

1

2

3

4

5

7

10

14

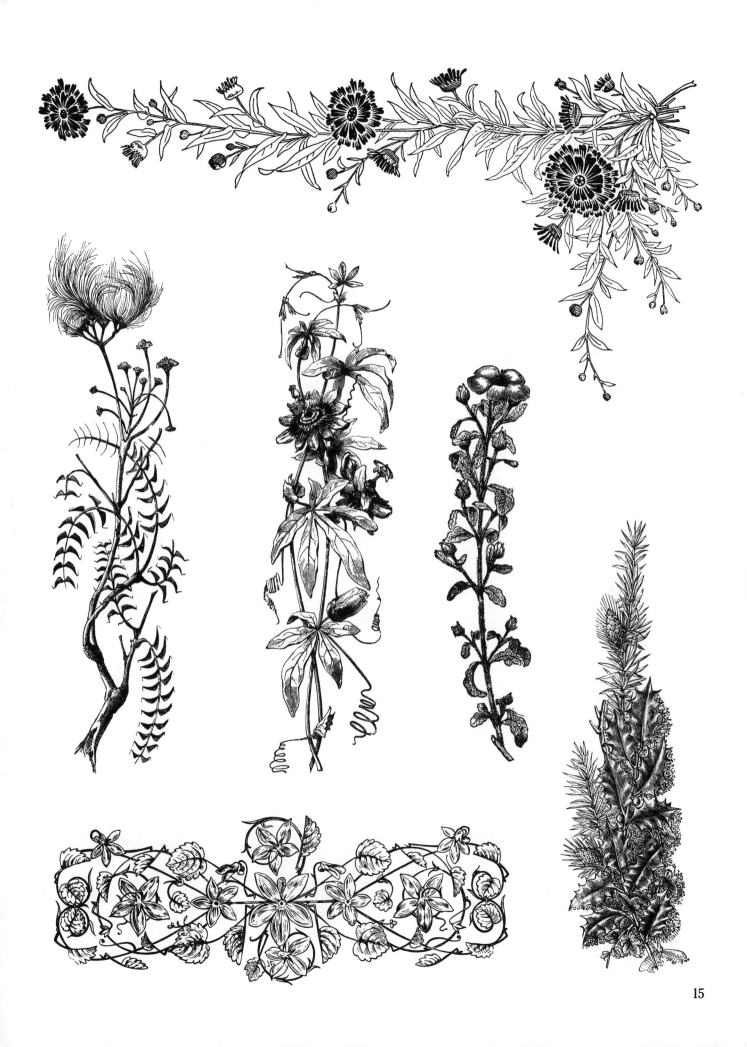

16

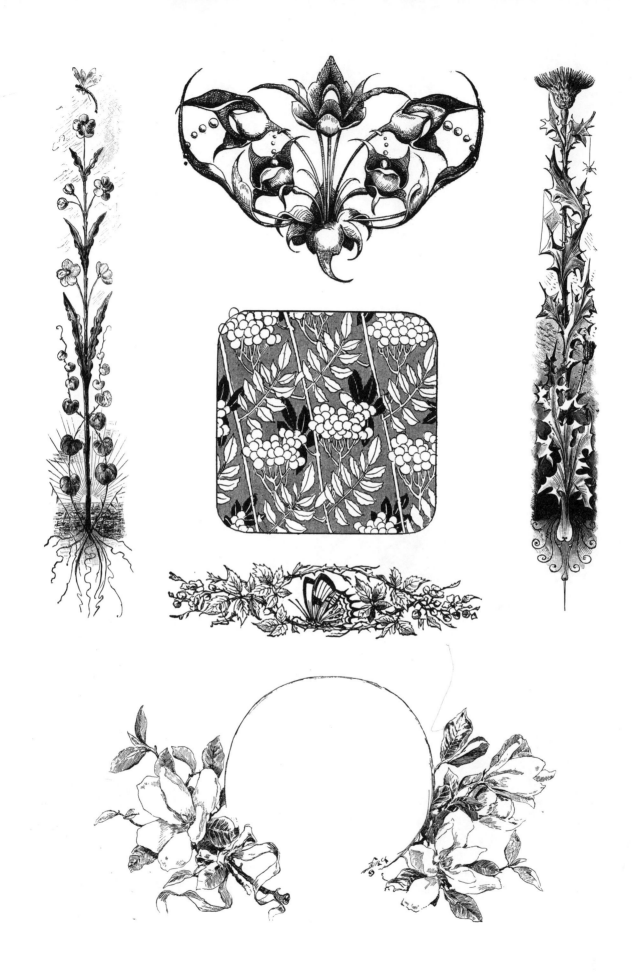

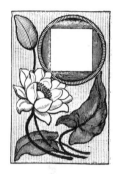

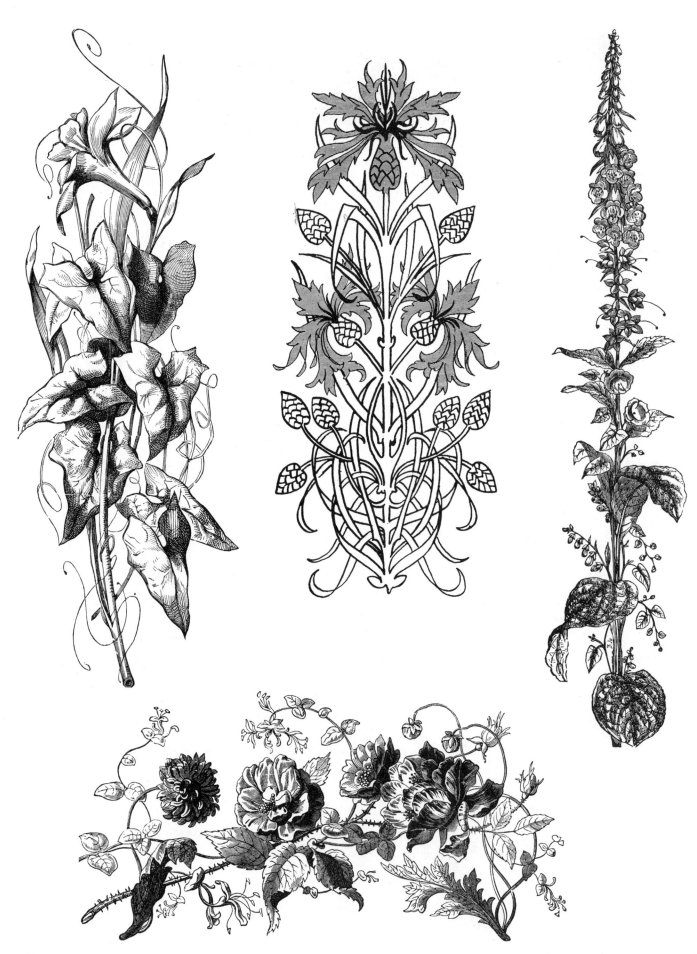

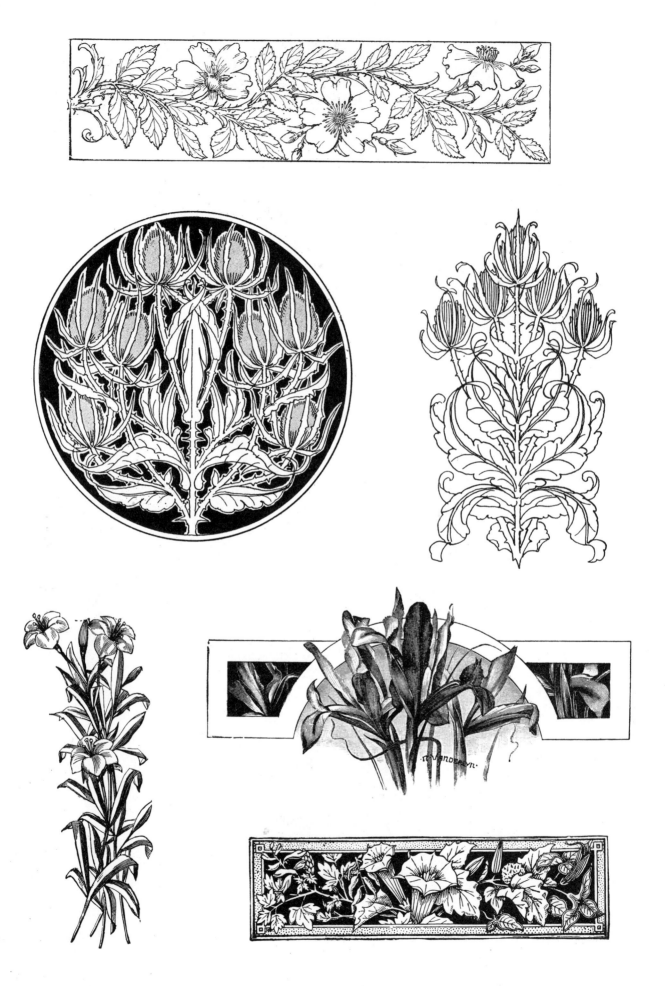

42

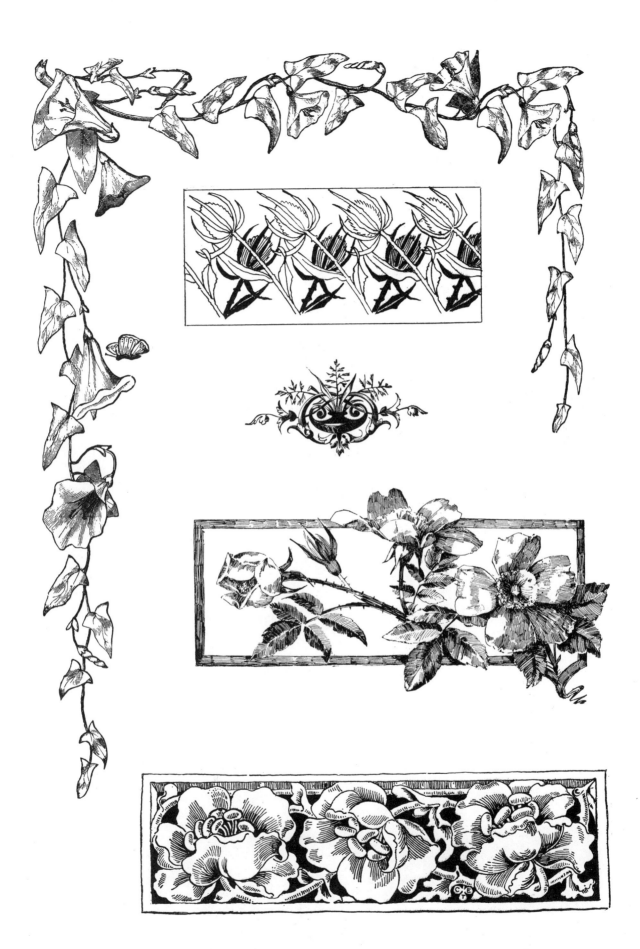

45

48

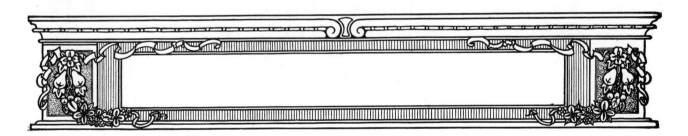

51

54

56

60

61

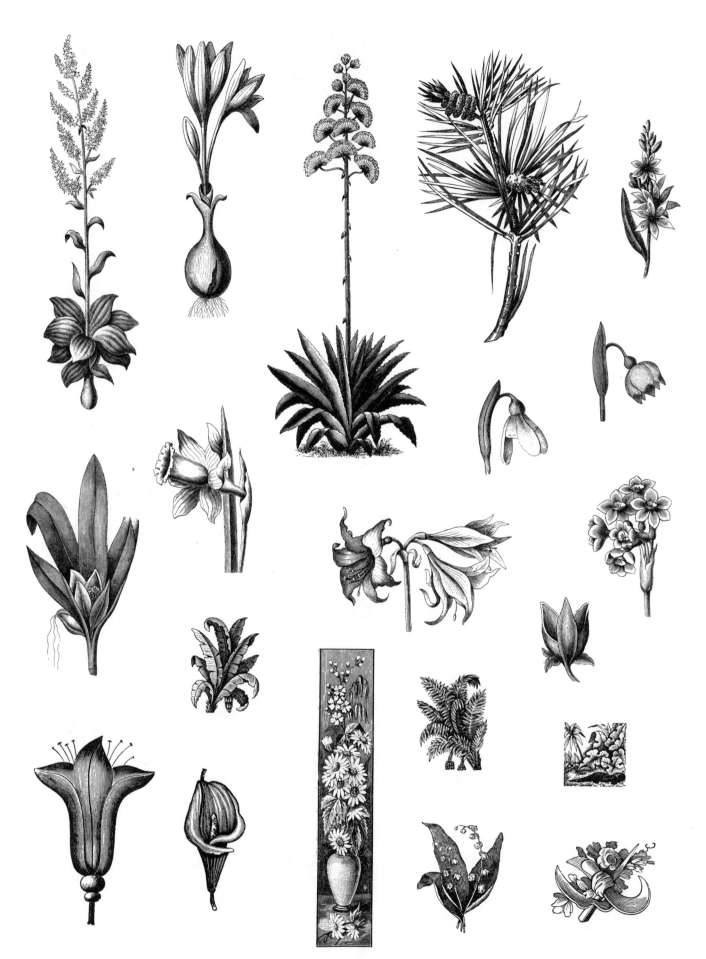

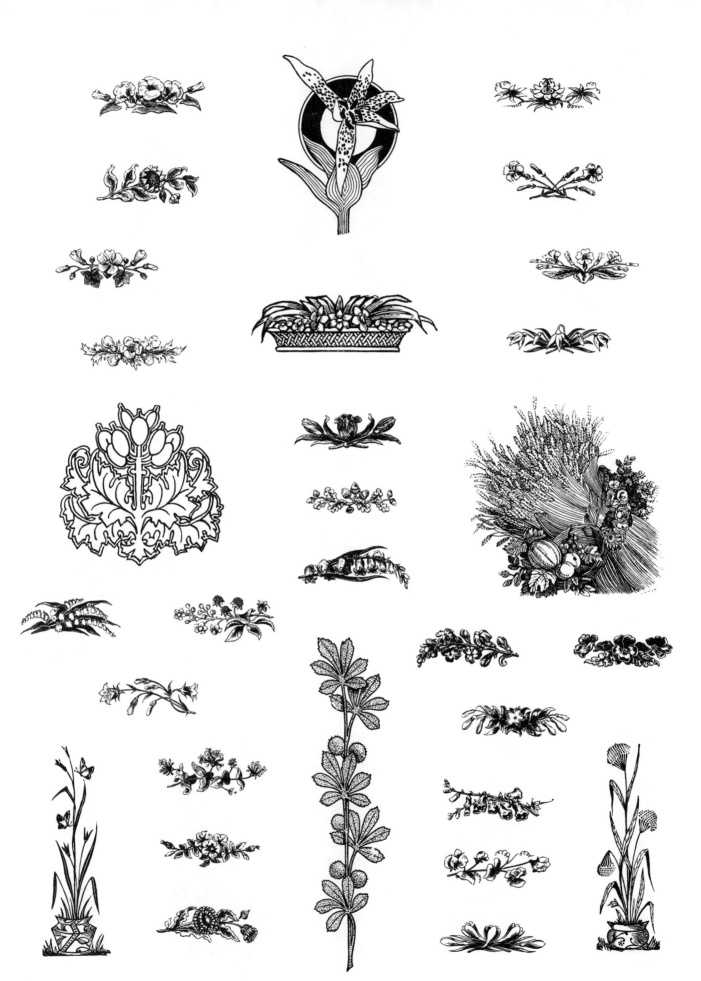

74

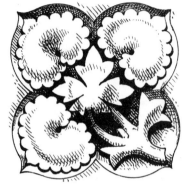

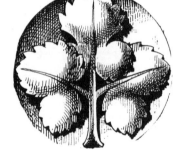

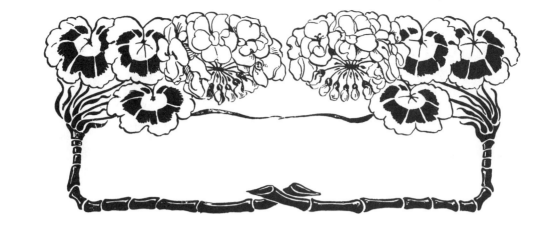

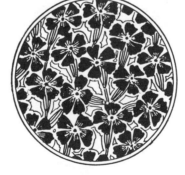

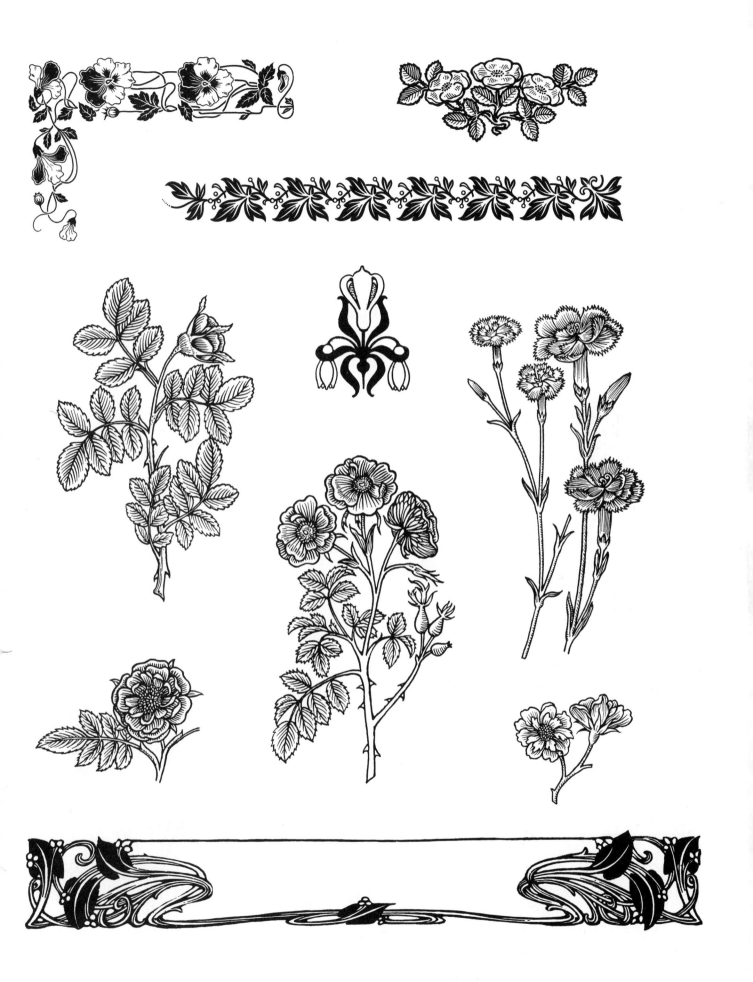

90

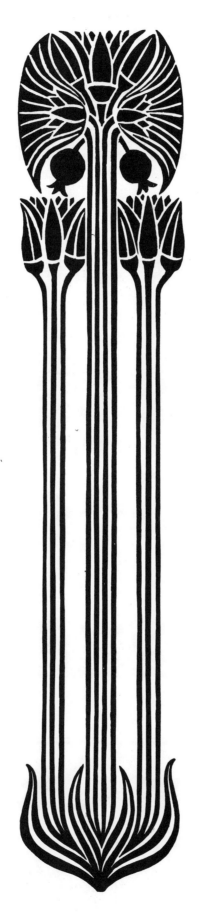

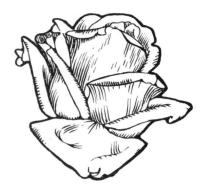

98

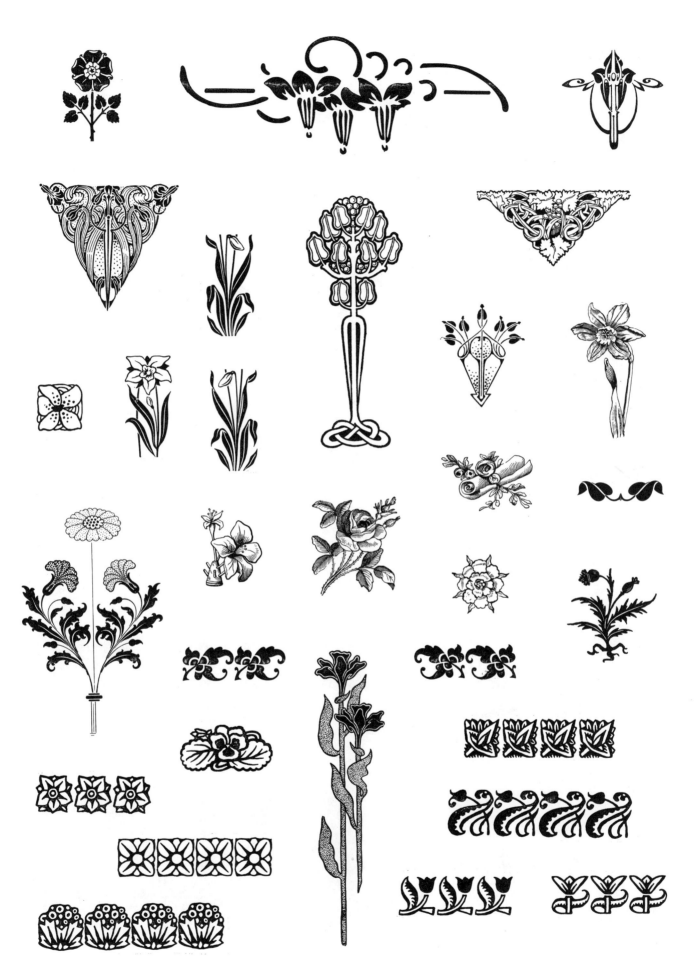

105

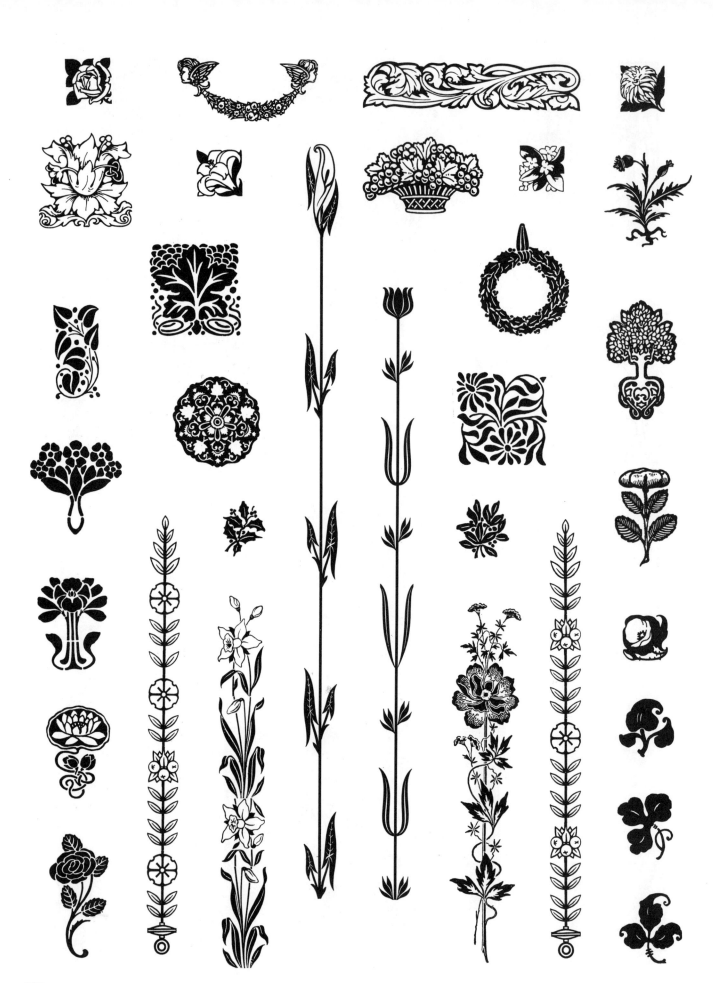

118

119

121